CW01656452

GREATEST FOOTBALL STARS

ACCESS THE ACTION!

Scan the QR code to hear this story for

FREE!

Published in the UK by Sweet Cherry Publishing Limited, 2025
Unit 4u18, The Book Brothers Business Park, Tolwell Road,
Leicester LE4 1BR, United Kingdom

Sweet Cherry Publishing Limited
Unit 31, The Pottery, Bakers Point,
Pottery Road, Dún Laoghaire,
Dublin A96 EV18, Ireland

SWEET CHERRY and associated logos are trademarks and/or registered trademarks of Sweet Cherry Publishing Limited.

2 4 6 8 10 9 7 5 3

ISBN: 978-1-80263-538-6

Greatest Football Stars:
Diego Maradona

© Sweet Cherry Publishing Limited, 2025

Text by Luke Paton
Illustrations by Sophie Jones

All rights reserved. No part of this publication may be reproduced or utilised in any form or by any means, electronic or mechanical, including photocopying, recording, or using any information storage and retrieval system, without prior permission in writing from the publisher. No part of this publication may be used or reproduced in any manner for the purpose of training artificial intelligence technologies or systems.

The right of Luke Paton to be identified as the author of this work has been asserted by them in accordance with the Copyright, Designs and Patents Act 1988.

This book is not authorised, licensed or approved by Diego Maradona. Any faults are the publisher's, who will be happy to rectify for future printings.

www.sweetcherrypublishing.com

Printed and bound in Turkey

FSC www.fsc.org MIX Paper | Supporting responsible forestry FSC® C111584

Sweet Cherry

DIEGO MARADONA

THE UNOFFICIAL STORY

WRITTEN BY
LUKE PATON

CONTENTS

1

A DIAMOND IN THE ROUGH

From the moment Diego Maradona was born on the 30th of October 1960, he was trying to kick a football.

The doctor handed the wriggling baby to his stunned parents, Diego 'Chitoro' Maradona and Dalma 'Tota' Salvadora Franco. 'Congratulations!'

he said. 'You have a healthy boy!'

Chitoro and Tota were over the moon, but they knew life wouldn't be easy now that they had five children.

Their house was no more than a shack in Villa Fiorito near Buenos Aires, Argentina. Chitoro had built it himself out of spare bricks and sheets of abandoned metal. He wasn't exactly a qualified builder, so the ramshackle house leaked whenever it rained.

Diego and his siblings had to share

one small room, and they all had to live without electricity or running water. The family were so poor that Diego only had one pair of trousers growing up.

Villa Fiorito wasn't a safe place to raise a family. It was a shantytown, meaning all the people who lived there had shacks and makeshift houses like Diego's. But the big problem was that it was full of criminals. The place was so lawless that even police were afraid to stay there overnight. It was also extremely

filthy. There were no sewers in the town, and very little sanitation. When Diego was only a toddler, he fell into a cesspit – a tank that collects raw sewage. As Diego's uncle helped him out of the pit, he said, 'Diegito, keep your head above the mess!'

It was sound advice for all of Diego's childhood. If he wanted to survive, he'd have to keep his head above the mess and get out of Villa Fiorito!

He started trying to make money as soon as he could to help his family claw their way out of there. Young Diego would rip the foil from old cigarette packets to try to recycle them. He'd collect scrap metal and try to sell it. He even opened taxi doors to help earn some money.

Ever since Diego was three years old, he knew that his best chance of escaping Villa Fiorito was through football.

His cousin Beto gave him his first football on his third birthday. Diego loved his new present so much that he slept with it!

The ball rarely left Diego's feet after that. He kicked it so hard and so often against one fence that the railings bent out of recognition, all before he'd even started school!

Diego was always practising his ball-handling skills. He did all kinds of flicks, tricks and keepy-uppies. He could keep the ball off the ground all the way from his house to his school, crossing a railway bridge along the way! When Diego couldn't play with his football, he'd do keepy-uppies with an orange or

screwed-up pages from a newspaper.

He played games of football on an empty plot of land near Villa Fiorito. Diego was a small boy for his age, and there were lots of other strong players who played in the matches. But Diego was better than all of them. He'd zip past anybody, even when they tried to foul him!

One of his best friends was a boy named Gregorio 'Goyo' Carrizo. Goyo was a great footballer too, and he'd started playing with a team called Los Cebollitas,

or the 'Little Onions'.

Los Cebollitas was the youth side of Argentinos Juniors – a big club that had a first team in the first division of the Argentine leagues.

One day Francisco Cornejo, the coach for Los Cebollitas, was thinking of finding new players to fill out his team.

Goyo said, 'Sir, I've got a friend who's better than me. Can I bring him next week?'

Cornejo was surprised. Goyo was an exceptional player, so if this new kid was better than him, he had to find out who he was. Cornejo told Goyo he'd be happy to see his friend.

Diego was only eight years old when he tried out for Los Cebollitas. But Cornejo had to pick his jaw off the floor when he saw Diego's skills.

He does things with the ball I've never seen in my life! he thought.

The ball looked as though it was glued to Diego's feet. He swept past bigger, stronger and faster players as if they weren't there. Diego was so good

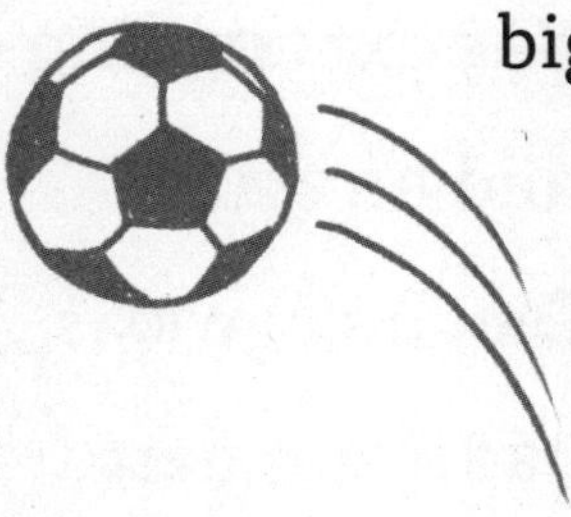

that Cornejo thought someone was playing a trick on him. *There's no way this kid is only eight years old! He seems to come from another planet!* he thought.

Diego tried to explain to Cornejo that he really was only eight years old, but the coach didn't believe him. He told Diego he had to bring his identification papers with him to the next training session to prove how old he was!

Immediately after Diego's age was confirmed, Cornejo made him part of the Los Cebollitas team. Diego and Goyo would get the bus together to go to the matches. They'd both play their hardest, but there was no denying that Diego was the star. Fans all over Buenos Aires began to hear about this small boy playing for Los Cebollitas.

Before long, Diego was entertaining the crowds at half-time during first division matches for the Argentinos Juniors first team. Fans loved his keepy-uppy tricks and flicks. They'd cheer for him

to carry on after the second half started!

Diego was mentioned in a national newspaper when he was only ten years old. 'He holds himself like a natural-born football player,' the newspaper raved.

He still wasn't earning money for playing football. After each game, Diego and Goyo would try to avoid paying for tickets on the bus on their way home, so they had some money left over for pizzas and cola!

But Diego wouldn't be skipping bus fares for very long. His talent was undeniable. He became so well-known that his coaches had to sneak the eleven-year-old Diego into matches for fifteen-year-olds. Even then, he'd be the best player on the pitch! The other coaches would get mad when they found out what had happened. 'Did you just play Maradona against me?' they'd scream.

A TV crew came to record Diego performing his sensational skills. 'I have two dreams,' Diego told them.

'To win the league and the World Cup.'

Argentinos Juniors believed he could make those dreams come true, and they signed him up after he turned eleven. They also agreed to rent an apartment for his entire family, which was only a mere few minutes from their stadium.

Diego's family cried when they saw their new home. It was in the capital city, and it was a real home with four walls and a non-leaky roof. They were finally out of Villa Fiorito!

I played football always thinking about buying a house for my parents and never going back to Fiorito, Diego thought.

If he could do that at age eleven, there was no telling what he could achieve in the future!

2

EL PIBE DE ORO

Diego made his debut for the Argentinos Juniors first team when he was fifteen years, eleven months and twenty days old. He wore the number 16 on his shirt, and he started the match on the substitute's bench.

Argentinos Juniors was losing 1-0

to Talleres de Córdoba at half-time. Coach Juan Carlos Montes approached Diego in the changing room.

'Are you up for it?' he asked Diego.

'Yes,' Diego replied. Strangely, he didn't feel nervous. He just wanted to play football!

'Go on, kid,' said the coach. 'Play like you know how. And if you can, nutmeg somebody.'

Diego took the instructions literally. He nutmegged Juan Cabrera from Talleres de Córdoba as soon as he had the chance!

The crowd loved it, although Cabrera didn't much like being embarrassed by a fifteen-year-old.

Diego didn't make any difference to the scoreline that day, but his debut performance had been fantastic. It was a sign of great things to come!

'Congratulations!' the other players told him. 'The defeat doesn't matter!'

Diego took off his number 16 shirt and shoved it into his bag. When he got home, he handed it to his mother as a souvenir. 'It felt like I held the sky in my hands,' he said.

Three weeks later, Diego scored his first goal for the club. It was the first of 115 goals he'd score in over five years and 167 appearances for Argentinos Juniors. The fans couldn't get enough of him! They called him El Pibe de Oro, which means 'The Golden Boy'. Argentinian supporters everywhere desperately wanted their new favourite footballer to play for Argentina at the World Cup in 1978.

They thought he was the best chance they had of making it to the final. But the only person who could make that decision was the Argentina coach, César Luis Menotti.

Menotti agreed to give Diego his international debut when he was only sixteen. Diego was great during the game, so he thought he had a chance of making it into the World Cup squad.

In the end, Menotti left him out of the final team.

'You are too young this time,' Menotti told Diego. 'But I think you will be the captain of the team in the next World Cup in 1982.'

Diego was crushed. He'd wanted nothing more than to play for Argentina since he was eleven years old! He told Menotti he understood and that he was happy to be the captain of the under 18s team ... but as soon as Menotti was gone, he started crying.

He sobbed his heart out, even while others tried to comfort him. They reminded him he was still very young for a professional footballer. 'You know how many World Cups you're going to play, right?' they said.

Diego didn't want to hear it. 'How do I tell my dad?' he cried. 'I'll never forgive Menotti!'

Diego stopped crying eventually ... but he never stopped being angry.

At first, he focussed that anger on playing even better football for Argentinos Juniors and the Argentina youth team. His excellence on the field led the Argentina U22s team to the final of the

1979 FIFA World Youth Championship in Japan. It just so happened Menotti was the manager of that team, too.

'Men, you are already champions,' Menotti told the U22s side before the final. 'I don't care about the result of this game; you have already shown you are the best in the world. No fouls or crazy stuff. Go out, play and entertain the 35,000 fans who are in the stands.'

The team didn't disappoint him. Argentina beat the Soviet Union

3-1 in the final, with Diego getting the third goal. It was his sixth goal of the tournament!

'That was the most fun I've had on a football pitch,' he laughed.

His incredible performances were enough to earn Diego the Golden Ball as the player of the championship. He'd officially arrived on the world footballing scene!

Argentinos Juniors couldn't hold on to Diego for much longer after that. He signed for Boca Juniors in

1981 and immediately had an impact. He scored two goals on his debut, and the team went on to win their league.

'It seems like a dream come true,' Diego said after his Boca Juniors victory.

But Diego was about to learn that sometimes dreams can turn into nightmares.

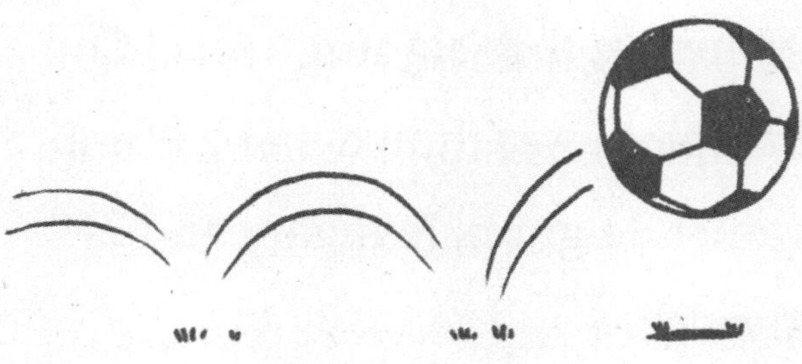

3

SEEING RED

The 1982 World Cup in Spain featured twenty-four international teams instead of sixteen for the first time. Argentina, the reigning World Cup champion, was drawn into a group against Belgium, Hungary and El Salvador.

The fans expected Diego to lead the team to another victory. They had good reason to think he could do this, too. In the run-up to the World Cup, Diego had signed for FC Barcelona for a record-breaking fee of £5 million. He was officially the world's most expensive player, and he was from Argentina!

Menotti was still the coach, and twenty-one-year-old Diego was an essential part of his squad this time around. Finally, he had a chance to show everybody how good he was on the world's biggest stage!

Unfortunately for Diego, his newfound fame also meant he had a target on his back. In the first game against Belgium, Diego was pummelled with harsh tackles – on and off the ball. He couldn't find any room to show off his skills, and when he did, he'd get brutally fouled.

'You get kicked wherever you play!' complained Diego.

The Belgians frustrated Diego so much that they snuck a 1-0 victory against the Argentinian side.

Unfortunately, their tactic of stopping Diego at all costs seemed to inspire the rest of the teams in the competition to do the same thing.

Diego found more space to delight his fans against Hungary in the second game. He scored two goals and helped his team win 4-1. But he was suffocated again against El Salvador and barely registered in Argentina's 2-0 victory.

Argentina went through to the second round, where their opponents were Italy. This time, Italian defender Claudio Gentile was charged with stopping Diego from playing the way he wanted to play.

Gentile took his job very seriously. He spent two days studying Diego and came up with a simple plan to get the better of him: follow Diego everywhere and never let him get the ball.

During the match, Gentile man-marked Diego all around the pitch and fouled him constantly, whether he had the ball or not. Diego complained to the referee so much that, in the end, Diego got a yellow card, not Gentile!

Gentile's tactics worked, too. Italy won the game 2-1.

Diego's anger at how he was treated by other players and referees boiled over in Argentina's last match of the tournament. It was against Brazil, and again Diego hadn't been able to influence the game with his usual flashes of brilliance.

In the 85th minute, Brazil's Batista fouled Diego's teammate Juan Barbas. Diego got mad and lashed out at Batista, kicking him in the thigh. The referee gave Diego a red card!

'What a tragic end to Maradona's

World Cup,' said commentator, John Helm. 'He's about to come and play in Barcelona, but this must be the most tragic moment of his career so far.'

Diego left the field fighting back tears. He wasn't sure whether he was crying because he was angry, upset or annoyed. It was probably all three rolled in together. He barely felt Alberto Tarantini hug and kiss him before he skulked down the tunnel.

4 KICKING OFF

Diego went to Barcelona with the dark cloud of the World Cup hanging over him. The fans knew he had the talent to be a big star – but they now also knew he had a terrible temper. Would he be able to control himself in La Liga, the greatest league in Spain?

'I am joining the club very happily and I will do everything to bring as many trophies as possible to the best club in the world, FC Barcelona,' Diego told the world after he signed his contract. He was determined to prove the doubters wrong!

In September 1982, Diego played his first competitive game for Barcelona and was phenomenal. He even got his name on the scoresheet!

Diego scored five more goals in his first thirteen La Liga matches! The Barcelona fans began

to believe he'd be the star everybody had hoped for!

But all was not well in the changing room. Barcelona manager Udo Lattek couldn't get along with his new star player. Lattek felt Diego had a big ego and wanted to be treated differently from the other players. Diego had constant fights with him!

He's not used to hard work, Lattek thought.

One time, all the other Barcelona players were ready to leave on the team bus to play an away game … except for Diego.

I have two options, Lattek thought. *Wait for Diego and lose my authority … or go without him.*

Lattek told the bus to leave without Diego. The players on the bus cheered the decision … but Lattek's relationship with Diego never recovered.

In fact, Diego wasn't happy in the Barcelona changing room until the club sacked Lattek. And when they replaced him with Diego's former Argentina coach, César Luis Menotti, Diego was thrilled.

Menotti knew how to get the best out of Diego. Essentially, it meant making the rest of the team revolve around him. Menotti went so far to please Diego that he scheduled training sessions in the afternoons so that Diego could sleep longer in the mornings!

Not everybody was happy about it, but Diego's football went from strength to strength. Under Menotti, Diego propelled Barcelona to victories in the Copa del Rey, the Copa de la Liga and the Supercopa de España. He scored thirty-eight goals in fifty-eight appearances, and one goal stood out among all others.

The memorable strike came against Real Madrid in Madrid's legendary Bernabéu Stadium. Diego picked up the ball in the Real Madrid half, dribbled towards the goal, swept past the keeper and was clean through. All he had to do was slot the ball into an open net.

But that was too easy for Diego!

Instead, Diego waited for a defender to close him down. Then, when the defender did a sliding tackle, Diego performed a superb dummy. The defender slid past him and straight into the goalpost! Only then did Diego pass the ball into the net.

It was so clever and cheeky that even the Real Madrid fans applauded the goal! The defender Diego had just embarrassed laughed as well.

But as good as Diego was, he could have given Barcelona so much more if not for one shocking encounter with Andoni 'Goiko' Goikoetxea.

Diego faced off against Goiko on the 24th of September 1983 when Barcelona took on Athletic Bilbao. The match was always destined to be fierce and physically challenging.

Two seasons earlier, Barcelona had marked Goiko as public enemy number one when he horrifically fouled Barcelona player Bernhard 'Bernd' Schuster. Schuster had to miss the rest of the season because Goiko severed a ligament in his knee!

Before this match, Barcelona fans boasted that their team played fluid, attractive football, while Athletic Bilbao were just too brutal. The Bilbao fans argued that Barcelona was pretentious and weak. Even the managers of the two clubs said nasty things about each other in the press!

The stage was set for an intense showdown at Barcelona's Camp Nou stadium – but nobody could have predicted what happened next.

Goiko was determined to stop Barcelona at all costs, of course. Throughout the game, his challenges were tough, verging on dangerous. He was still taking chunks out of

Diego even when his team had no hope of winning.

'Take it easy, Goiko!' Diego begged him. 'Chill out, you're losing 3-0 and will just get booked for nothing!'

Goiko paid him no attention.

Then Diego got the ball inside his own half, facing the Barcelona goal. He had no way of seeing Goiko thundering towards him. The Athletic Bilbao player lunged at Diego from behind, his studs smashing into Diego's leg just above the ankle.

CRASH!

Diego went down in a heap.

That sounded like a piece of wood cracking, thought Diego.

Diego rolled on the ground in pain. The medics were called over, and he had to be taken off the pitch on a stretcher extremely carefully.

The ligaments in Diego's ankle were damaged. He could hardly move it. It would take months of rehabilitation and some metal pins for him to recover.

Yet Goiko only received a yellow card from the referee for the challenge!

A disgusted Menotti

called the Bilbao players 'anti-footballers'. An English newspaper went further, giving Goiko the nickname 'Butcher of Bilbao'.

The rivalry between the two teams got out of control after that. Barcelona met Athletic Bilbao again in the 1984 Copa del Rey final. Before this encounter, Bilbao's manager called Diego 'stupid' and said, 'It's a shame a player like him who earns so much money has no human qualities whatsoever.'

Menotti shot back, 'Barcelona is

prepared to respond to a determined violence with the same violence.'

The final was not a pretty match.

There was cynical play from both sides, and more fouls than shots on goal. Diego got another wallop from Goiko, and the referee issued seven yellow cards during a frustrating ninety minutes for both the fans and the players.

In the end, Bilbao was the winner … but that wasn't the story everybody was talking about the next day.

After the final whistle, Bilbao player Miguel Sola gave Diego an obscene gesture. Diego saw red.

He ran over to Sola and kicked him in the face. Sola was knocked out cold, and a massive fight suddenly broke out on the pitch. Players from all sides joined in the fight in a disgraceful scene. It took riot police to calm everybody down.

Following the match, Diego was banned from playing football in Spain for three months. But Diego didn't stick around to serve his ban.

His time in Barcelona had come to a terrible end.

5

THE NEW KING OF NAPLES

Diego signed for SSC Napoli for another record-breaking fee of £6.9 million. The fans in Naples, Italy, fell instantly in love with him.

75,000 people bought tickets to watch Diego walk into the team's Stadio San Paolo for the first time.

Diego put on quite a show for them, too.

He arrived at the stadium in a helicopter. He could hear the fans screaming, 'Ho visto Maradona, ho visto Maradona!', which means: 'I saw Maradona, I saw Maradona!'

They love me, thought Diego. *They really and truly love me.*

Diego stepped out of the helicopter wearing blue trousers, a white T-shirt and a Napoli scarf. The supporters knew he was wearing the colours of his new club!

As he strode out to the middle of the pitch, they chanted, 'Olé! Olé! Olé! Olé! Diego! Diego!'

Naples is crazy! thought Diego. *As crazy as me! How can I let them down?*

He blew kisses to the fans and waved to as many people as he could. Somebody gave him a ball, and he performed a few keepy-uppies and curled the ball into one of the Napoli goals. The crowd roared.

'Good evening, Neapolitans!' Diego said after being handed a mic. 'I am very happy to be with you!'

He volleyed a ball into the stands next and screamed, 'Forza Napoli!' This means: 'Come on Napoli!'

But behind the scenes, Diego knew he had his work cut out for him.

Napoli was close to the relegation zone when he joined. It was going to take all his skill and leadership to pull them out of their years-long slump.

Their mentality is about avoiding relegation, he thought. *This year will be different.*

It strangely helped Diego that there was a massive north-south divide in Italy at the time. The football clubs and supporters in the north of the country hated the clubs and supporters from the south of the country. Diego's team, Napoli, was from the south.

The atmosphere was extremely hostile when Napoli played against the most powerful team in the north, Juventus. Their fans sang horrible songs to the Napoli fans.

'You are the shame of the whole of Italy!' they sang.

'Wash them! Wash them! Wash them with fire!' they sang.

They called Napoli supporters and players the 'unwashed' and 'peasants'.

It made Diego angry. And when he was angry, Diego played football even better!

Diego led his team to an eighth-place finish in his first season at Napoli. In his second season, the team finished third.

He scored thirty-one goals across both campaigns. Some of them were so good that they sent the fans into a craze. Diego especially liked the one where he bested the Lazio goalkeeper from forty yards out!

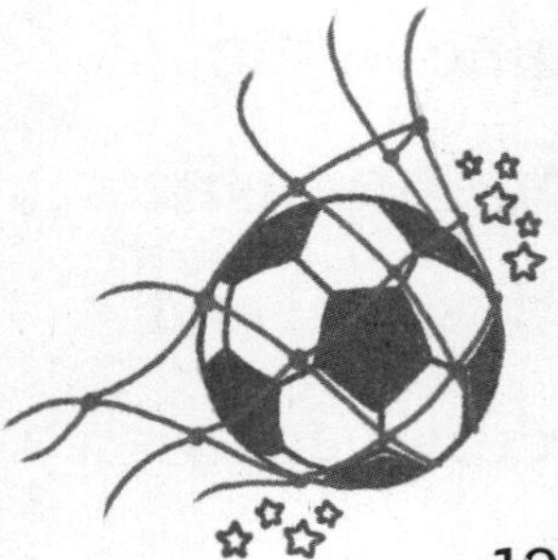

But the sweetest victory came against Juventus. In November 1985, Diego scored a stunning free kick that was enough to defeat their northern rivals 1-0. The excitement in the crowd caused five people to faint and two to have heart attacks!

The celebration in the changing room was just as manic. 'The colour of today's goal is blue, blue for the people of Naples,' Diego told the press. 'Because no one who doesn't live in Naples can imagine all the stuff people were saying during the week. For this reason, this goal and this victory have been deserved by the people.'

Manager Ottavio Bianchi saw Diego as their most important playmaker.

'It would be a mistake to deploy you in a merely tactical position,' he told Diego. 'You must be left to express yourself as best you can. It's up to us to create a concrete block around you, to highlight these qualities.'

Now Diego didn't have to worry about defending while playing for

Napoli. His only objective was to make goals and score goals!

His third season with Napoli was when everything fell into place.

Diego scored seventeen goals in forty-one matches, and Napoli won the Serie A championship. It was the first time a southern team had ever won the title!

On the day the team clinched victory, Diego led the team on a lap of honour around the stadium. 'This is the greatest moment in my life, honestly!' Diego exclaimed. 'I've won a few things, but the problem is that I didn't win it in my country, you see? Napoli is my home. My home for sure!'

The team went wild in the changing room after the match. They were up on the tables singing and dancing. They chanted: 'Oh mama mama mama! Oh mama mama mama! Do you know why my heart is racing? I've seen Maradona! I've seen Maradona! And mum! I fell in love with him!'

TV crews tried to interview the team, but Diego took over

those duties as well. He kissed and hugged his teammates and friends. But when he tried to say something sensible, his team played a prank on him and covered him with water!

Fans of Napoli loved Diego so much that they changed the words of the Lord's Prayer to honour him: 'Our Maradona, Who Takes the Field, We have hallowed thy name, Thy Kingdom is Napoli, Lead us not into disappointment, But deliver unto us the title, Amen.'

Thanks to this championship win, Diego was the new king of Naples.

6

THE HAND OF GOD

Diego had missed out on the 1978 World Cup for being too young. He'd been disappointed in his performances in the 1982 World Cup. So when the 1986 World Cup rolled around, Diego was determined to be at his best.

'I hope this can be the Maradona World Cup,' he said. 'I really want it, with all my strength, because if this is the Maradona World Cup, this will be Argentina's World Cup, and we both want that.'

This World Cup was going to be played in Mexico at a high altitude in conditions just right for Diego to thrive. But when he arrived at the Argentina team's base camp near the Azteca Stadium in Mexico City, Diego was not impressed.

Their bedrooms were unfinished and

uncomfortable. Some players had to buy their own lampshades. They had one telephone and one TV for everybody to share!

But the dingy lodgings actually made the team stronger. It meant they had to share everything and spend all their time together. Diego's father was there to fire up the BBQ and feed all the players with Argentinian meat that had been specially flown in. The team acted like a family, creating strong bonds between them.

The players also discovered all sorts of superstitions. One player had to shave at the same time before every match. The manager had to phone home at the same time before a game. Diego's superstition was making an invisible player on the floor of the changing room using boots, socks and a shirt.

Argentina beat South Korea 3-1 in their opening game, so Diego decided he had to make that same invisible player before every game. The others carried on doing their strange superstitions, too!

Diego scored a goal in the 1-1 draw with Italy next, and he was a critical player in Argentina's 2-0 win over Bulgaria. Then a 1-0 victory over Uruguay in the second round set up a quarter-final match against England.

It was a very testing time for Argentina to play England. In 1982, four years before this World Cup, Argentina and England had fought in the Falklands War against each other. The conflict lasted for ten weeks, ending in the Argentinians surrendering to

England. Sadly, many people were killed in the fighting.

The press told anybody who'd listen that this 1986 World Cup clash between Argentina and England was going to be like another Falklands War. England's football fans hardly helped the matter when they started chanting, 'Bring on the Argentines, we want another war!'

But the football teams tried to keep everybody calm. 'We're here to play football,' England manager Bobby

Robson said. 'Don't confuse the two issues.'

'It's just football, full stop,' agreed Diego.

Anyway, Diego and his side had a more pressing issue before they played England. They needed to find a new football kit!

The players thought the kit they'd played Uruguay in was too heavy to deal with the heat in Mexico. So Argentina's backroom staff had to search madly throughout Mexico City to find a new one. The one they found was a bright blue colour.

'Oh no, not that one,' said coach Carlos Bilardo. He hated the look of it!

But then Diego walked in and smiled. 'What a nice shirt this is, Carlos,' he said. 'With this one, we will beat the English.'

'OK,' replied Bilardo, sheepishly. 'Let's go with this one.'

England knew all about Diego by this point, of course. But their manager, Robson, wasn't overly concerned.

'Don't worry,' he told his defenders.

The match was notorious for showing two very different sides of Diego's talent: his cunning and his genius.

In the 51st minute, English midfielder Steve Hodge attempted to clear the ball away from the box, but accidentally kicked it back towards his own goal. The ball looped up into the air towards the goalkeeper, Peter Shilton.

The 1.83 metre-tall goalie rushed out to collect the ball safely. He was challenged by the 1.65 metre-tall Diego. There should have been no contest. After all, Shilton could use his hands to reach even higher than Diego.

Without thinking, Diego stretched out his arm and used his hand to hit the ball before Shilton could get it. The ball bounced towards the England goal and rolled into the net, leaving the crowd stunned.

The English players waved their arms, appealing for handball.

Diego looked at the linesman.

The action happened so fast that the

linesman didn't see me putting my hand in, he thought.

The referee looked at Diego ... and gave the goal!

English players swarmed the referee, screaming to him that it was handball. They thought the goal should be disallowed!

But Diego and Argentina celebrated in front of their fans.

That's symbolic revenge for the war! Diego thought.

There was no instant replay and no VAR in those days. The match officials had given the goal, and the goal was going to stand. No amount of complaining would help England now.

Diego knew he'd handled the ball – and the millions of people watching at home knew it as well – but he said nothing. Even after the game, he played it down, 'That goal was scored a little bit by the hand of God and another bit by Maradona's head.'

The moment went down in history as the 'Hand of God' goal and is still considered the worst call in any World Cup.

But the second goal Diego scored against England was an absolute masterclass.

It came just three minutes after the Hand of God goal, while England was still reeling from the baffling decision.

England's Glenn Hoddle was dispossessed in the Argentinian half. José Luis Cuciuffo passed it to Héctor Enrique, who swept it to Diego. Diego was still in his own half, facing his own goal. Then he zipped to the right and left two England players, Peter

Beardsley and Peter Reid, chasing shadows.

Diego had the option to pass to Jorge Burruchaga, but he kept the ball instead. He slipped past Terry Butcher next, and all of a sudden, he only had the goalkeeper to beat. Diego feinted, taking the keeper out of the way. As Butcher tried to chop him down in desperation, Diego slotted the ball into the net.

It was the 'Goal of the Century'!

The other Argentina players ran after him, shouting, 'What an amazing goal!'

Argentinian commentator Víctor Hugo Morales screamed, 'Genius! Genius! Genius! Ta-ta-ta-ta-ta-ta-ta! *Goal!* I want to cry. What an unforgettable run! A cosmic kite. What planet did you come from so that the whole country is a clenched fist shouting for Argentina?'

The England manager had to grudgingly admire Diego's incredible goal. England striker Gary Lineker had to stop himself from applauding.

'I've scored the goal of my life!' Diego cheered.

'I believe that he demonstrated that he is the best player in the world,' the coach said. 'I think he is a true idol!'

Argentina won the game 2-1.

'Diego! Diego! Diego!' chanted the crowd.

Diego cried and kissed the Argentina shirt.

There were now only two games between him and the World Cup trophy!

7

WORLD CUP '86

Argentina met Belgium in the semi-final.

Diego was so pumped to get the match going that he fouled someone within the first seven seconds of play. But after that, he played the game of his life. The crowd delighted as he moved the ball effortlessly around the park with backheel flicks, blind passes, a rabona and a few dummies.

But when the score was still 0-0 at half-time, Diego was furious.

He gathered his team in the tunnel and ripped them to pieces. He told them the Belgium side was arrogant because the Argentinians were playing badly. 'We need to change our attitude!' Diego warned.

The other players felt Diego's anger, and they were terrified of letting him down. When the second half

began, they were in no doubt they had to start playing better.

If we're to win this game, Diego thought, *I'm going to have to come out and win it alone.*

In the 51st minute, Diego scored another sublime goal. Latching onto the end of a pass from Burruchaga, he flicked the ball past the Belgian keeper.

Goal!

His second goal of the match came twelve minutes later. This time it was down to another flash of Diego's brilliance.

He rounded three defenders with ease, then chipped it beautifully into the back of the net. 2-0!

Diego and Argentina were going to the World Cup final!

In the changing room after the game, the team was ecstatic! They stripped off their shirts and jumped on the tables. The singing and chanting were deafening!

'The best footballer in the world was born in Argentina!' someone screamed.

Diego shouted back, 'We're all together! Together, we are whole!'

He started singing with the team: 'Argentina's gonna be the champion!'

'We'll keep this moment in mind,' Diego said. 'The thing is, nobody believed in us, and I think we showed all the defeatists who wished the worst for this team. Now that we are here, we don't want to miss the opportunity we have to be known all over the world.'

All that stood between them, and World Cup glory was West Germany. The game was scheduled to take place in the Azteca Stadium in Mexico City on the 29th of June 1986. 114,000 fans piled into the grounds to see what magic Diego could perform.

In the tunnel before kick-off, Diego marshalled his troops. 'Here we go! Come on!' he told them. 'Let's go with everything we've got! Two hours! In two hours, we're going to be the champions! Let's go and kill them!'

The other players took strength from his belief. They were ready to do whatever it took to win!

'West Germany is not scared of us,' Diego reminded them. 'They have a better track record than us. They are going onto the pitch with more confidence. They think we are going to chicken out!'

As the players stepped out onto the field, the crowd was chanting, 'Argentina! Argentina! Argentina!' as a band kept the beat.

The atmosphere was electric. Both sides wanted to win, but only one could be crowned champion of the world!

Argentina started the game better. In the 23rd minute, they earned a free kick on the right wing. Burruchaga whipped the ball in, and the German keeper misjudged its flight. He came out to catch it and missed it completely. That left a wide-open net for José Luis Brown to head it in!

It got worse for the Germans in the 56th minute. Argentina's Jorge Valdano finished off a smart move by slotting the ball neatly past the stranded German goalkeeper. It was 2-0, and things were looking good!

But fifteen minutes from time, West Germany hit back. The captain, Karl-Heinz Rummenigge, headed his first goal of the tournament in the

74th minute to make it 2-1. Then Rudi Völler pulled West Germany level with nine minutes of normal time to go.

Diego was distraught. How had they let this happen? There were still nine minutes of the game left to play, and he was worn out!

I'm exhausted, he thought. Then he looked at the opposition team. *But the whole of the German defence are exhausted too. I need to be the number 10 the fans expect me to be.*

Three minutes after the German equaliser, Diego got the ball in the centre of the pitch. He looked up. There were two West Germany players thundering towards him. Two more were crowding him nearby.

But just beyond them, Burruchaga was making a run behind the defence. Diego knocked the ball beyond his markers and found Burruchaga in acres of space.

That's the best pass of my career, thought Burruchaga.

He took one touch ... two ... then shot with the third ... the ball flew past the keeper and

slammed into the

bottom corner.

Goal!

Argentina did it!

They beat West Germany 3-2!

They were the world champions!

The crowd burst into tears of joy!

Diego went wild!

His teammates hugged, kissed and applauded.

Everything they'd ever dreamt about had come true!

Diego led his team up to the podium to collect the trophy.

'The world's greatest player receives

the world's most important football prize,' said the commentator.

Diego kissed the World Cup trophy and hugged it tightly to his chest. He never wanted to let it go. When he raised it to show the crowd, they tore the roof off the place with their cheers!

The team performed a lap of honour, and the players raised Diego on their shoulders as their king. They knew if it hadn't been for him, they wouldn't have won the World Cup.

In the 1986 World Cup, Diego scored five times and set up another five goals. He was a crucial part of ten goals for Argentina in this tournament – and the team only scored fourteen! Diego was officially awarded the Golden Ball for being the best player of the championship.

The first thing Diego did after the celebrations died down was phone his mother.

'Hola, Mama!' he said.

'Hola, my love,' replied Tota.

'Tota! I love you, Mama.'

'My life! My life.'

'I love you lots, Mama.'

'I love you too. Go rest, my son. Today you made me the happiest mother on Earth!'

'I never dreamt of anything that's happening to me,' Diego said.

It was the greatest moment of his entire life.

He'd never again feel so good.

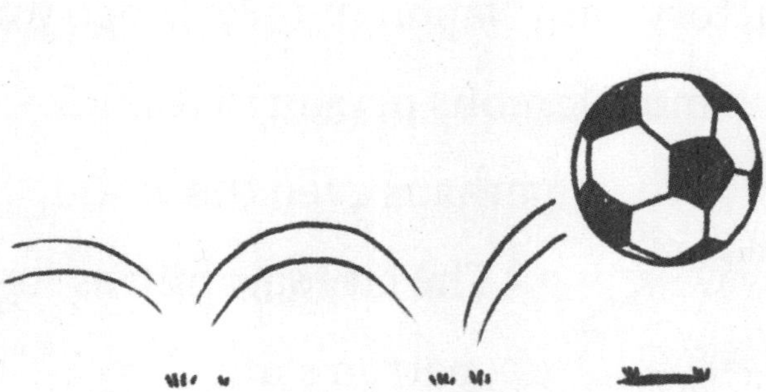

8

DIEGO DIVIDED

After his World Cup victory with Argentina in 1986 and the Serie A victory with Napoli in 1987, Diego was the most famous person in Naples – perhaps even the world. The city saw him as its patron saint.

But Diego was beginning to find their love a bit too much.

'Everywhere I go there is a commotion,' Diego complained. 'I can't go shopping, to the cinema, to the theatre.'

The moment he stepped outside, he'd be mobbed by fans wanting to kiss him, touch him and get his autograph. He needed security guards just to get him through the crowds of fans to his car.

Hundreds of mothers named their newborn babies after him.

People wrote songs about him. They sold Diego wigs and figures, and carried them everywhere they went. One time, Diego had a blood test and the nurse stole a vial of his blood to put in a church. It was like he was some sort of god!

'I don't understand people who think I am more important than their mothers or even God,' Diego said, confused.

But as much as Diego complained about the clinginess of the fans, he also loved being the centre of attention. His personal trainer, Fernando Signorini, said it was like there were two different people inside Diego.

'There is Diego and there is Maradona,' Signorini said. 'Diego is a kid who has insecurities, a wonderful boy. Maradona is the character he came up with to face the demands of the football business and the media. Maradona can't show any weakness.'

The problem was that the more time Diego spent in Naples, the more often he was 'Maradona' and not 'Diego'.

Signorini started to worry about him losing his way.

'With Diego, I would go to the end of the world,' he told Diego. 'But with Maradona, I wouldn't take a step.'

'Yes,' replied Diego, 'but if it wasn't for Maradona, I'd still be in Villa Fiorito.'

'Diego, be careful,' was all Signorini could think to say.

Whether Diego or Maradona, he was still playing incredible football for Napoli. Diego showed off his mesmerising

control of the football in one famous warm up against Bayern Munich in 1989. He did keepy-uppies with his knees, his feet, his head and even his shoulders. He kicked the ball high and controlled it with one delicate touch. He looked like a boy enjoying football in his back garden, not the world's most famous man about to play in the semi-final of the UEFA Cup!

He led his team to more trophies, including the Coppa Italia in 1987 and the UEFA Cup in 1989. It was the first

time Napoli had ever won a major European trophy! Diego also became the highest ever scorer for Napoli with 115 goals.

'We are on top of the world!' the supporters said. 'We are the best in Europe!'

But Diego wasn't happy.

He found the love of the city too much, and his personal life was in shatters. He was beginning to feel Naples was bad for him.

He brought this up to the Napoli chairman, Corrado Ferlaino. 'I have nothing left to do,' Diego said. 'I want to end my career somewhere calmer.'

Diego still had a contract with Napoli that tied him to the club until 1993. But Ferlaino made Diego a promise. If they won the 1989 UEFA Cup, he could transfer to another club.

When Napoli won that trophy on the 17th of May 1989 against Stuttgart, the team and Ferlaino started celebrating on the pitch. But Diego wouldn't let Ferlaino forget his promise.

'This is proof that I know myself better than anyone!' Diego told Ferlaino. 'And this is the down payment to be allowed to live my life! I want to live my life, please.'

'I don't want to sell you, Diego,' Ferlaino replied. 'I want you to stay here at all costs.'

Nothing could convince Ferlaino otherwise. Diego was shocked. He took his complaints to the press. 'I no longer have the focus and mind to play in the Italian league,' he said. 'It is not a matter of money.'

Even when Diego refused to rejoin

Napoli for training at the start of the 1989/1990 season, Ferlaino insisted his star player would stay with the club. Diego was forced to spend another year with Napoli against his will.

'When it'll please Corrado, I'll play,' an angry Diego told the press.

Somehow, amid all the off-field drama, Diego and Napoli won Serie A for a second time at the end of the 1989/1990 season. From the outside, it was the greatest run in the history of the club!

Yet Diego's life was going off the

rails. After every match on Sunday, Diego would go out to eat and party with his friends … and he'd keep partying until Wednesday! Then he'd cleanse and train until Sunday, before starting the whole routine again. He was suffering from terrible lower back pain and needed five injections before every game just to get moving.

It was an unsustainable life. If he carried on this way, there'd be no Diego and no Maradona!

He thought the only way out of his downward spiral would be getting the chance to lift the World Cup again.

The 1990 World Cup was going to be played in Italy – the very country that had been his home for seven years.

But if Diego thought this was a good sign, he was sadly mistaken.

9

THE FINAL WHISTLE

'I want to enter history,' Diego said. 'As a madman, no one can beat me.'

His motivation to win the World Cup in 1990 was at an all-time high. He called on Signorini, his personal trainer, to get him into the best shape possible to support his team during the campaign.

'We'll work out every day,' Diego told Signorini. 'We'll spend morning, afternoon and evening together.'

He sprinted on a treadmill until he could barely walk. He lifted weights until his arms felt numb. He was more committed than ever before, and the results started to show.

Diego lost a stone in one month. 'There is not one ounce of fat,' he boasted to Signorini.

Signorini agreed. 'You've recovered the speed and reflexes that make you such

a special player,' he said. 'You're ready to cause all kinds of problems for the other teams!'

But five days before the World Cup, Diego had a massive blister on the big toe of his right foot. He also had a niggling ankle injury, and he wasn't the only one in the Argentina squad struggling. Burruchaga and Óscar Ruggeri were also suffering injuries.

These setbacks made most people think Argentina had no chance of winning the 1990 World Cup.

But the critics should have known Diego thrived when the odds were against him. If anything, these challenges made him want to win the World Cup even more!

He knew it would be tough, though. Diego played football in Italy every week, but he wasn't welcomed by the Italian fans during the tournament. They booed the Argentinian national anthem before their first match against Cameroon, and cheered when Cameroon won the game 1-0.

Diego was very angry. After everything he'd done for Italian football, this was how they treated him!

Argentina limped through the group stage, qualifying for the next round by the skin of their teeth. It was much the same story in the knock-out stages.

Diego provided an assist for their 1-0 victory over Brazil in the round of 16. Then the quarter-final against Yugoslavia finished a dismal 0-0 and went to penalties.

It was Diego's job to take the third penalty in the shoot-out. It could have put his team up 3-1 ... but he clipped it at the perfect height for the Yugoslavian keeper to save!

Diego was gutted. He sent up a silent prayer, then wished his goalkeeper, Sergio Goycochea, good luck.

'Take it easy, monster,' said Goycochea. 'I'm going to save two more.'

Goycochea did exactly that! Argentina went through 3-2 on penalties

to set up a semi-final against none other than Italy.

This match was going to be the real test for Diego.

As fate would have it, the semi-final was played at the Stadio San Paolo, where Napoli played their football. So Diego would be playing for Argentina in his home stadium in Italy against Italy. It was a strange situation!

But Diego saw an opportunity. He remembered all the times he'd played for Napoli against Juventus or the teams from the north of Italy. He remembered how they'd looked down on the supporters and called them 'unwashed' and 'peasants'.

Diego knew at least some Napoli fans would be supporting him, and not the Italy international team. So he tried to get even more of his Napoli fans on his side!

'The Neapolitans are being asked to be Italians for one night, while the other 364 days of the year they get called names,' Diego told the press.

'I know they are Italians; we cannot ask for them to cheer for us, but the rest of Italy should know the people of Naples are just as Italian as they are.'

His comments caused widespread outrage in Italy. People wondered how Diego could possibly ask Italians to support Argentina in a game against Italy played in Italy?!

One banner at the game read: *MARADONA. NAPLES LOVES YOU, BUT ITALY IS OUR HOMELAND.* Another one read: *DIEGO IN OUR HEARTS, ITALY IN OUR SONGS.*

Despite this, lots of fans still cheered for Diego.

When he jogged out into the stadium, there was a roar of approval from the supporters. They didn't boo when the Argentina national anthem played, either. It was almost as if the teams were playing for a neutral crowd, and that worked to Argentina's advantage.

The match itself wasn't one to remember. It finished 1-1 after extra time.

For the second match in a row, Argentina needed

to win on penalties to go through.

The first six penalties all found the back of the net. It was 3-3 when Italian player Roberto Donadoni stepped up to take his spot-kick.

But Goycochea, the Argentinian keeper, was still on sparkling form from the previous round. He saved Donadoni's penalty!

Diego was next.

If he scored his penalty, Italy would be on the brink of going out of their home tournament.

The fans would hate him.

The stadium would turn against him.

But Argentina would also be close to getting through to the final.

What would he do?

'It's a screaming hell in the stadium,' said the commentator.

Diego placed the ball on the penalty spot.

He waited for the referee's whistle.

Then he ran forward and side-footed the ball past the keeper.

He scored!

Argentina was 4-3 up.

Italy's Aldo Serena had one chance to rescue Italy. He needed to score his next penalty or Italy was out of the tournament.

He ran up to the ball, struck it hard and ... Goycochea saved it!

Argentina was through, and Italy was out!

The stadium went silent.

Fans buried their heads in their hands and started to cry.

Diego was ecstatic on the pitch ... but the backlash against him was almost immediate.

'Maradona is the devil,' ran a headline in the Italian press later.

'The obnoxious one,' they called him.

'Lucifer lives in Naples,' they said.

Suddenly, Diego was the most hated person in Italy.

When Argentina played in the 1990 World Cup final against West Germany, the crowd started booing their national anthem again. The Italian crowd desperately wanted West Germany to win!

Diego was furious his anthem had been disrespected, but for once, he wasn't able to channel that rage into a spectacular performance. The final was a terrible match. Some say the worst World Cup final there's ever been. Argentina had two men sent off, and West Germany scored a penalty to win 1-0.

Afterwards, Diego told everybody there was a conspiracy to make Argentina lose. 'The penalty didn't exist,' he moaned. 'It was given just to let the Germans win.'

But it didn't make any difference.

His World Cup was over.

His time in Italy was over.

And he didn't know it yet, but the peak of his international and club football career was over, too.

It was the end of the Maradona era.

10

LEGACY

On the 25th of November 2020, Diego sadly died of a heart attack at sixty years old.

His passing had a massive effect on the world of sports.

'What sad news,' said footballing legend Pelé. 'I have lost a great friend, and the world has lost a legend.

There's still so much to be said, but for now, may God give strength to his relatives. One day I hope we can play football together in the sky.'

'It's a very sad day for all Argentinians and for football,' agreed Lionel Messi. 'He leaves us, but he doesn't leave us, because Diego is eternal. I will keep all the beautiful moments I lived through with him.'

Cristiano Ronaldo added, 'Today I say goodbye to a friend and the world says goodbye to an eternal genius.

One of the greatest of all time. An unparalleled magician. He leaves too soon but leaves a legacy that has no limits and a void that will never be filled. Rest in peace. You will never be forgotten.'

The president of Argentina, Alberto Fernández, announced the country would have three days of mourning for Diego. 'You took us to the top of the world,' he said. 'You made us immensely happy. You were the greatest of them all. Thank you for having existed, Diego.

We're going to miss you all our lives.'

Football matches around the world observed a one-minute silence in the days after his death.

Napoli football club renamed their stadium the Stadio Diego Armando Maradona in honour of their greatest player.

Thousands of fans flocked to the stadium to pay their respects to Diego. The same thing happened at the Boca Juniors stadium in Argentina.

Diego will always be remembered as one of the greatest players to ever kick a football. But in his home country of Argentina, he's seen as something more than a human.

In 1928, a man named Borocotó, the editor of a newspaper called *El Gráfico*, wrote about what the embodiment of Argentinian football would look like. He said it would be a young boy 'with a dirty face, a mane of hair rebelling against the comb … His stance must be characteristic; it must seem as if he is dribbling with a rag ball.'

He was describing Diego decades before he was born!

Diego came from nothing and achieved the greatest prizes in international football. He was and continues to be an inspiration for any small boy who's ever enjoyed kicking a football.

Diego never saw himself as a god, though. When asked how he'd like to be remembered, he said, 'A good father and the best player ever.'

The debate about who is the best footballer is likely to go on for another hundred years. Diego? Pelé? Messi? Ronaldo?

Fans will point to Diego's dazzling skill with the ball, his deft touch, his ability to win games single-handedly and the 'Goal of the Century' against England in the 1986 World Cup.

All these things and more mean Diego will be talked about for as long as people talk about football.